# SONG OF THE NIGHT CROW

## Christopher J. Roe

POETRY

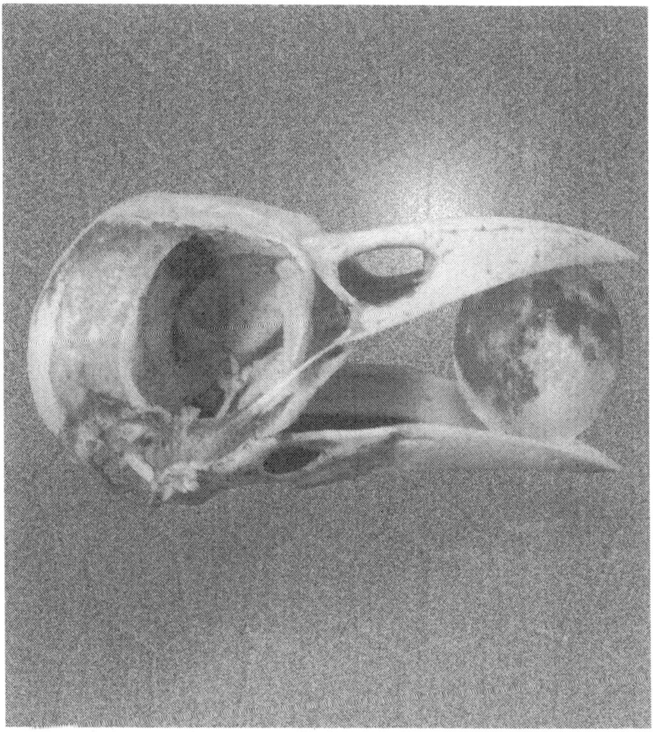

## Books by the Author:

**Poetry**:

*Tricia's Song*
*Misé Eire (I am Ireland)*
*Words Alone, Late in Coming*
*Inside Out*
*Off the Deep End*
*The Fire That Split the Stone*
*Wounded Dove*
*The Skipping Stone*
*The Workman's Bicycle*
*The Collector*
*Give My Regards to the Moon*
*In the Song of Every Bird*
*Song for the Ordinary Man*
*Persistent Vision*
*On Days When Dreams Are Not Enough*
*Mona Lisa's Bones*
*Clouds & Days*
*Scenery & Interiors*
*Eternal Cloud of Self*
*Ashes of Sacrifice*
*Something From Nothing Comes*
*Bits and Pieces of a Broken Life*
*Language of the Light*
*The Shaping of the Clay*
*Undercurrents*
*Through the Forest to the Light*
*Interrupted Journey*
*Out of Body ~ Out of Mind*
*The Light I Cannot See*
*Echoes in the Stones*
*Mosaic*
*Should I Be My Own Undoing*
*The Imaginist*
*Murmurations*
*Down To the River*
*Song of the Night Crow*

**Collections**:
*TalonQuest*
*Papa's Poems*
*Re:verse*
*Awakening*
*Re-Awakening*
*Rapture of the Muse - Volumes I, II, III, IV and V*
*Warren Peace*
*Lotus Eater*
*The Fire of the Muse*
*Dead of Winter*

**Memoir**:
*Dead Rainbows*

**Fiction:**
*Death of a Poet*

*Song of the Night Crow* - written and designed by Christopher J. Roe
Cover Photo: Photoshopped Stock
Author's photo by Michael Cevoli

*Contents © 2015 by Christopher J. Roe*

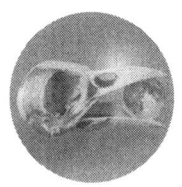

# SONG OF THE NIGHT CROW

## Christopher J. Roe

POETRY

Stone Heart Press • 27 State Street • Warren, RI 02885 U.S.A.
e-mail: stoneheartpress@yahoo.com

# Contents

| | |
|---|---|
| I Suppose | 1 |
| Lately I've Been Thinking | 2 |
| The Leaving | 4 |
| Darkness of Unknowing | 8 |
| Questions | 9 |
| Starlings | 10 |
| The Silent Poet | 12 |
| Prayer of Pain & Peace | 13 |
| Scavenging | 16 |
| TGIF | 18 |
| Art Is Life | 19 |
| Steeplechase | 20 |
| As the Crow Flies | 22 |
| Museum of the Everyday | 23 |
| Limits | 24 |
| A Quiet Day In Nature In Harmony With Birds | 25 |
| The Calling Sea | 26 |
| Human Fault | 28 |
| Where the Wolf | 30 |
| Ain't It Just the Truth | 32 |
| Remnants | 33 |
| The Poet and the Priest | 34 |
| Alive and Kicking | 36 |
| Gone to Bangor | 38 |
| Simply Complex | 39 |
| Song of the Night Crow | 40 |
| The Fledgling | 42 |
| Gray Day Introspection | 44 |
| Fingers and Lips | 45 |
| Nutshell | 46 |
| Day On the Bay | 47 |
| Into the Vortex | 48 |
| Oblivious | 49 |
| Unwinding | 50 |
| Beauty Is | 52 |
| The Gambler | 53 |
| String Theory | 54 |
| Last of the Summer Roses | 55 |
| Twenty-five Shades of Gray | 56 |
| Island In the Sun | 58 |

| | |
|---|---|
| What Occurs | 60 |
| Liquid Sky | 61 |
| The Heresy of Now | 62 |
| The Rocker | 63 |
| My Age Is Winter | 64 |
| How Now | 65 |
| Tower Builders | 66 |
| Knee Jerks | 68 |
| Vacuous Vacuum | 69 |
| The Fourth | 70 |
| Leonardo | 71 |
| Something | 72 |
| Alphabetical | 74 |
| What Was Easy | 75 |
| Shopping Cart | 76 |
| Half-Light | 77 |
| Becoming | 78 |
| Flagstuff | 80 |
| Questions of Loneliness | 82 |
| Only the Lonely | 83 |
| In the Mirror World | 84 |
| The Following | 86 |
| The Pink Screen | 88 |
| Big Lesson | 89 |
| Dark Soul | 90 |
| Mid | 91 |
| As the Mind Sighs | 92 |
| The Greater Question | 94 |
| Boiler Room | 96 |
| Cyclopean | 97 |
| A Religious Experience | 98 |
| Of Flowers and Love | 100 |
| Privilege & Power | 101 |
| The Running Man | 102 |
| The Large Barking Dog | 103 |
| The House of Love | 104 |
| Versus | 105 |
| Last of the Diehard Smokers | 106 |
| A Modern Man | 107 |
| Passion & Persistence | 108 |

*For the ladies
of the Hail,
the most helpful
of all librarians*

## I SUPPOSE

You took yourself out last night
spent all that time and money
now you wonder why you can't get it right
    I suppose you think that's funny

Tonight you'll watch the art shows you missed
the skies and your life no longer sunny
and now you regret getting pissed
    I suppose you think that's funny

Always thinking of the one you love
so bright and sweet as honey
she's what you're always thinking of
    I suppose you think that's funny

She's far away and that makes you sad
now for no reason your eyes are always runny
because you lost the best thing you ever had
    I suppose you think that's funny.

## LATELY I'VE BEEN THINKING

Lately I've been thinking
been thinking my whole life long
thinking about doing the right thing
to make up for all the wrong

I've been thinking a lot about life
been thinking too about love
can't no one make me stop
except the one above

Thinking makes me happy
sometimes thinking makes me sad
but thinking about you baby
is the most fun I've ever had

Power of thought can move mountains
it can change the way you live
but to sit there thinking nothing
is a sin I can't forgive

I think about you thinking about me
and thought folds itself into thought

and lately I've been thinking
it's some rare disease I've caught

I think a lot about not thinking
and take a pill to get some sleep
but dream about God, life, death, and love
and other things not quite as deep

I think that thinking is a form of art
and I haven't thought my masterpiece yet
at night I think my most profound thoughts
that in the morning I forget

Most of all I think about love
which can be ruined by over-thinking
and when I feel that coming on
is when I turn to drinking

Love will take care of itself — or so I think
but I may have messed it up — and so I drink
and when drink has my mind out of synch
I can feel the icy hand of death — or so I think.

## THE LEAVING

I came to the village
just four years ago
I came for peace and quiet
myself to get to know

I made a few friends
at least they seemed to be
but when I needed them
they weren't there for me

I was never meant to live
by anyone's rules
especially those
proposed by fools

With all my time
I get to think a lot
with all my time
I get to drink a lot

It's the abject loneliness
that I find hard to take

and the smile I show
is the one I fake

I have accomplished much
and I did it all by myself
say all the paintings on the wall
and all the books on the shelf

But I haven't done
all that I need to do
and a decision must be made
in the absence of you

My future lies
beyond the ocean wide
where I will go to discover
and not to hide

I will continue doing
the things I do well
drinking a lot and
being lonely as hell

*Continued >*

And those I leave
who may feel betrayed
time will heal their wounds
and the scars will fade

And in that land
beyond the sea
I hope to find the who
I am meant to be

It's no one's fault
that I don't belong
and I'm not saying
you did anything wrong

I have been adjusting
to what I will become
the one who marches
to a different drum

Whether I die here or die there
it matters not

it will be the end
I've always sought

I've left behind
enough of myself
just look at the wall
and look at the shelf

So remember me
those I leave behind
I never meant
to be unkind

You are always in my heart
and on my mind
but the truth is still
out there for me to find

And as I depart
on my final quest
remember, I always tried
to do my very best.

## DARKNESS OF UNKNOWING

Your day has come
your day has gone
the train has been moving
since you got on

The day you could have seized
went past the window in a blur
and every turn of the wheels
takes you further away from her

Will the day come again
will you be ready to leave the train
will you know the station when it comes
will there be an ending to your pain?

The rhythm of the rails brings sleep
and dreams of what you've lost
the life you gambled away
and the coins that you tossed

Making wishes that didn't come true
now sadness is like the whistle blowing
destroying existence with its mournful sound
and you weep in the darkness of unknowing.

## Questions

Last night I found myself walking through
my dark apartment answering questions the TV
was asking. *Do you want a new car?* No. *Are you
healthy enough for sex?* Yes. *Constipated?* No.
It was obvious the TV didn't know me very well,
so I turned it off and turned on a light knowing
that my home security was lacking, and I am
probably using the wrong shampoo, and how I'll
be burdening my loved ones with final expenses
by dying without burial insurance. I feel so sad.
It appears that my insides might be filled with
purple solids and blue liquids wreaking havoc
on my inner workings. But there is a machine
that will cure me by making me walk uphill in the
comfort of my own home. I know I'll have to talk
to real people soon. I can feel reality slipping away
and I know I'll only get one chance to get it back.
Tomorrow is Monday. A new week is starting
and, if I'm lucky, a new life too, if only the TV
will stop asking so many fucking questions.

## STARLINGS
*for Calvin Kahn, 1959 – 2015*

Sky darkly dominated

by starling's rhythmic swarm

water is the color of tears

and the air is chilled

like when a soul disappears

and there is a sense of death

hovering at the edge

of awareness and thoughts

that erupt like startled fish

in the mind's vast ocean

amid the search for meaning

in the weakness of a wish

as a few drops of rain

fall and stain the bench

with random polka dots

and I ponder, as I often do,

at the suddenness of life

and the abruptness of death

and the randomness of it all

where there is a breath

and then no breath

to fuel the soul

and the heart gives up

surrendering the body

to the earth of its birth

and the vacuum created

slowly fills with

the dust of time

and starlings again

command the sky

and rain's tears stain

the waters of memory

randomly.

## THE SILENT POET

The tongue languishes in his mouth
an atrophying muscle unused
a wealth of words untapped
the poet in silence, confused

Conversation a forgotten art
the poet at a loss for the word
he sits in the silence of his thoughts
reticent, aloof and reserved

The words of others mock him
though they speak of nothing at all
their voices harsh in the still air
he retreats behind his silent wall

He knows he has so much to say
but there is no one to say it to
so he puts it all in books
that no one reads, though they say they do

But as a poet he feels incomplete
for a poet to succeed he must be heard
he knows well the joy of writing
but the voice gives power to the word.

## Prayer of pain & peace

*Pain of living*
  *Peace of death*
*Soul departs upon a breath*

The way unclear
The danger near
Shadows dance behind the objects of the sun

A truth denied
No path untried
And the river never falters on its run

Seduction's trap
No one leaps the gap
The flag of loneliness stirs in the breeze

Strength is waning
No use complaining
There exist greater problems than these

*Pain of living*
  *Peace of death*
*Soul departs upon a breath*

Nights of solace
Days pile upon us
The time has come for the traveller to choose

*continued >*

Does love still exist
What have I missed
Is it true that a loser must always lose?

Why must there be trial
Why must there be denial
Shouldn't love be the best reason to live?

Mistakes were made
The scars will fade
If the wounded heart can somehow forgive

*Pain of living*
   *Peace of death*
*Soul departs upon a breath*

With no one to please
I get up off my knees
But discover there is no place left to go

If the truth be told
I have grown old
And what I knew I now no longer know

As the body fails
The future pales
There is not much left that you can cling to

Sand through fingers
Only memory lingers
And for the life of me I haven't got a clue

*Pain of living*
   *Peace of death*
*Soul departs upon a breath*

Life is bare bones
I've tossed the stones
But nothing can be read in the runes

The heart has felt
The hand was dealt
There is no judgment on the faces of the moons

Nothing left of me
Nothing left to be
And life is growing dark around the edges

My spirit growing thin
Nothing left to lose or win
Only the echoes of passion's pledges

*Pain of living*
   *Peace of death*
*Soul departs upon a breath.*

## SCAVENGING
*in memory of Spalding Gray*

There are things I used to do

that now I do no more

for the times that were

are times now gone to me

the propriety of age being what it is

I console myself with drink

And since the accident in Ireland

my thoughts have not been my own

and the search for who I am

is more a scavenger hunt

than introspective self-examination

or even drunken epiphany

I wonder why it happened to me

as if compulsiveness was mandatory

the truth is; it's all about the story

the journey is the tale twice told

as if once heard it can be buried

in the dark world of the worms

With dreams of water and floating

a sensual sense of serene flight

between worlds of chaos and freedom

an end to confessional writing

just the nothingness of peace

and the otherness of eternity

Riding the ferry back and forth

on the estuary of a misbegotten life

with only one destination, only one desire

the aimless drifting of non-thinking

the ultimate blankness of verse

uncoupling the couplet

What is scavenged from the trash

becomes the collective truth

defining the every from the what

and the shadow from the sun

like the things I used to do

that now I do no more.

## TGIF

Today is Friday. TGIF.
That used to mean something
back when time was divided
into a series of two-part sections;
minutes and hours
days and nights
weeks and months
years and the blink
of an eye that is life itself,
divided into two worlds;
work and leisure;
work days and weekends.
But there are neither now
only the world of linear time
that exists for creating.
Week days, holidays, vacations
now just a streaming tide of thought
with its inevitable highs and lows.
And all my time filled with wonder
enjoying the art of others
and painting and writing poetry
while searching for the soulful
inspiration for both.
And in the constant flow of time
I celebrate a different TGIF;
The Good Inspiration Found.

## Ars est vita

It is not what you see
but how you see it.

• 

In the moment that
art is, you are.

• 

You are not creating art
but interpreting existence.

• 

The artist retains
the soul of a child.

• 

And in that innocence
lies the ability to love.

• 

And in the art
the ability to live.

## STEEPLECHASE

The blue flag drops
and the horses bolt
stallions and mares
and even a colt

Around the big tree
in the middle of the field
the thunder of hooves
but no horse will yield

Over bracken and bush
over rails and fences of stone
and along the sandy beach
race the pied and the roan

Steeple to steeple
beside the windswept sea
the horses run without a care
back to the flag topped marquee

The great race is on
the whole village turned out
the gentry sipping their tea
the rest drinking whiskey and stout

There is music and song
it really is quite a fete
with victory for one
and for the rest, defeat

Horses race with all their might
until the race is finally run
the party lasts late into the night
until no one remembers who won.

## AS THE CROW FLIES

I get to the point
as the crow flies
that is to say
with great effort
and exertion.

•

Nothing comes easy
everything is difficult
unlike a swoop through space
on the rush of wind.

•

They say a crow
flies in a straight line
meaning, I suppose,
it would circle the earth
back to where it started.

•

And so it lands
to rest and eat
before taking off
in a new direction
and in that way only
does it get to where it's going.

•

In a way, I am like the crow
I get to my point,
rest and eat,
before taking off
in a new direction.

## MUSEUM OF THE EVERYDAY

Hidden in the Museum
of the Everyday is a
half chewed wad of gum
preserved as a metaphor
for impatience.

In a glass display case
the last cigarette butt
the last smoker extinguished
just before dying
of cancer.

On a wall of oil paintings
hangs the blank canvas
of your ambition
and lost among wrapped mummies
is the sarcophagus of your love.

And well preserved
in a terra cotta coptic jar
is your broken heart
still beating in it's belief
of undying love.

And the crumpled foil
gum wrapper in the ash tray
is like the shed skin
of the snake you used to be
somewhere back in the day.

## Limits

I write poetry

to the limits of my attention.

Most art is limited in some way

either in its creation

or in its appreciation.

Voice is an imperfect instrument

communication is interpretive

and seeing can be deceiving.

All that really matters

is what is retained

without explanation

and not intellectually

but emotionally.

That is what defines art

and it is unfortunate

that most art exists for the few

while the many participate

to the limits of their attention

but without retention

it is meaningless.

## A QUIET DAY IN NATURE
## IN HARMONY WITH BIRDS

A quiet day in nature

In harmony with birds

Swooping swallows

Lofty in their grace

Osprey family calling

From their tripod home

Egret, on stilts, stalking

The exposed mud bank

Stately Blue Heron

Surveying its grassy realm

Sparrows, Gulls, Terns

And Pipers all enjoying

The environment

Of the marsh that

They, and we, share

That I am trying to

Capture on canvas

So in my small way

I too can sing.

## The Calling Sea

*There exists in me*
*some link to the sea*
   *like some vague, forgotten*
      *family history.*

1

Maybe a distant

whale boat captain,

or Civil War service

on the Monitor or Merrimack,

or maybe some distant

pirate blood is calling.

2

But the sea keeps

calling out to me

with its seductive song

and salty seaweed smell

and its breezes, waves

and moon tugged tides.

3

But I am a landlubber
and I don't know how
to handle these feelings.
Is it a calling, or merely
the hubris of wanderlust?

4

But the breeze beckons
the gulls nag and urge
the tides swell and surge
and the soul lets loose
its billowing sails
and I surrender to
the siren's call.

*There exists in me*
*some link to the sea*
    *like some vague, forgotten*
        *family history.*

## HUMAN FAULT

The formal gardens in the sun
possess a certain beauty
with islands of organized color
and hedges tied in knots

But like hundreds of nudes posing
it is only an imitation of life
using life itself as material
but still it is not a masterpiece

And when it is done and the models
begin to dress, the scene comes alive
in its beautiful random dance
becoming the beauty of life itself

Mankind marveled at all the stars
filling the heavens, but couldn't resist
connecting them with imaginary lines
creating a zodiac of constellations

As if stars alone are not beautiful enough
we need to imagine them as beasts

with mystical powers to explain the life
we can't explain and so seek to change

Individuals fall in love with other individuals
and immediately begin changing each other
until they are a couple, a new dynamic
that either works or fails as beauty fades

Why is it when we find ourselves in an Eden
we feel the need to change it to suit our desires
we must tempt fate because it is there
and it must be made to fit our concept of life

The apple is not beautiful enough
we must taste it and crush it into cider
and drink it to alter our own reality
because we fear its wild beauty

We just can't leave well enough alone
we can't accept Nature for what it is
our wildness that we have suppressed
is manifested in our human fault.

## WHERE THE WOLF

In the camera's flash
her eyes burned red
the wolf's a yellow fire

Fur the color of ash
and a feeling of dread
mixed with desire
- •

The eyes to the soul
either warm or cool
in the sudden light

Each in their role
the fear of the fool
for teeth that bite
- •

One is young, one old as night
in a blurred photograph
a moment frozen in time

One feels hunger
one afraid to fight
the subtle difference sublime
- •

A tiger or a lion
can be trained
to be a circus act

But wolves rely on
instincts ingrained
avoiding human contact
•
Wildness is their only reality
kept in zoos, they go insane
and their eyes burn

Individuals with a pack mentality
yet with a single-focus brain
what they could teach if we would learn
•
And what they dream of
is not performing in a tent
you'll never seen one in a circus

They howl at the moon for love
surely they are not so different
these wolves from us.

## AIN'T IT JUST THE TRUTH

Lover gotta love
Hater gotta hate
None of us agree
    And
So we must debate

No one can be right
If everyone is wrong
Music is fleeting
    But
Singers own their song

Life ain't black or white
Most of it is gray
If no one listens
    Then
Who cares what you say

Lover gotta love
Hater gotta hate
Most who come to know
    Have
Mostly come too late.

## Remnants

The day breaks
and the clouds fall
into pieces of rain
and the dew is brewed

And the broken day
with its sharp edges
baking in the sun
melts into the night

Moon a half mirror
of reflected light
the stars exploded
millions of years ago

Curdled dreams in sleep
invoke the damages of age
and the holy art of distilling
tries to mend the spirit

Wounded heart still beats
old scars soften into flesh
breath like pallid ghosts
hangs on the cold night air

And I gather up the pieces
of my shattered existence
a broken man picking
through life's remnants.

## THE POET AND THE PRIEST

The poet said to the priest,

"You are as vague

as the smoke of a distant fire,

but not as bright."

The priest replied, "I am

but a servant of God,

a doer of his bidding."

"You prove my very point, priest."

And each, entrenched in their belief,

tried to stare each other down

in the brittle silence.

The priest smiled, "It is the will of God."

The poet wearily shook his head,

"Your collar is your announcement

at the pulpit of your pronouncements

you who cast the first stone of judgment."

The priest sighed, "My son,

you have gone astray and lost your way

on the road to the promised land."

"And whose promise is it?"
the poet asked. "And if I
do not believe in the promiser
what good is the promise?
As pointless as this conversation
would be my guess."
And with that, they fell silent
and the silence felt eternal
until the priest said to the poet,
"I yet hope I shall see you
in heaven one day, poet."
The poet laughed, "If that
were to come true, then it's I
who would see you in that hell
of our creation, priest."

## ALIVE AND KICKING

Out of the gallons
of blood they've
drained from me,
out of the probing,
of growths and polyps
they've scraped out,
and the X-rays, EKGs
CAT scans and MRIs,
there must be something
they can tell me
about myself.
But they say I'm fine,
with the added caveat;
for a man of your age.
And then they write
prescriptions for pills.
Seven at last count,
nine really, but I stopped
taking two that made me
feel sick and dizzy.
A clear case of the cure
being worse than the disease.
Diseases they will not name.
Am I then merely
a collection of my symptoms?

# SONG OF THE NIGHT CROW — Christopher J. Roe

A healthy man riddled
with mysterious pains.
Losing things day by day;
hair and teeth and memory
and the ability to walk.
I do not see the need to pray.
I have the ability to kneel
but not the ability
to get back up.
Most of my bodily functions
are proving to be unreliable
and my mind, such as it is,
is beginning to wander.
My heart has a murmur
caused by a hardening valve
and there is no pill for that.
Their only diagnosis
is that I suffer from
the vagaries of old age.
It is that vagueness
that has me worried.
That these aches and pains
are merely painful reminders
that in spite of it all, I am
still alive and kicking.

## Gone to Bangor

And all of beauty gone to Bangor
silence settles like a shroud
distant future of music calling
where loneliness is not allowed

And in the song the heart's alive
and with the music time can heal
when the sands of solitude shift
the future begins to reveal

And through the suns and moons
of passing time's differing light
I watch the silent boats leaving
riding moonlit wakes of white

And time passes oh so slowly
with neither mood nor anger
while in the dark, patience bleeds
for all of beauty gone to Bangor.

## SIMPLY COMPLEX

I am a simple man
in a complex way
stripping life to the bone
living day to day
I don't have much
but it's almost enough
no matter what you own
it's just plain old stuff
I write and I paint
it's about all I do
remembering a time
when love was new
but now living alone
in formless solitude
interrupted occasionally
by a pleasant interlude
and you can call it love
or blame it all on drink
whatever you call it
it what makes me think
its not about drunkenness
and it's not about sex
it's about how I became
so simply complex.

## SONG OF THE NIGHT CROW

The crow came to me in the night
and pecked at my useless lips
I could see it coveting my eyes
in the darkness by the crypts

The crow stared at me intently
its gaze the deep dark of an abyss
wing tips resting lightly upon my face
as soft as a lingering kiss

The crow did not speak to me
from its perch upon my chest
like some dark Morpheus
summoning me to my final rest

The crow was the black of absence
absolute darkness of a total eclipse
its eye an unblinking moon
heralding the apocalypse

# Song of the Night Crow — Christopher J. Roe

The crow flew to the open window
causing the curtain to stir like a ghost
then it flew into the night calling back
*"The devil take the hindmost"*

The crow fled my now chilly room
leaving me to ponder its parting words
and I lie here dismissing its wisdom
as the mere folly of talking birds

The crow offered up its wisdom
but did I really want to know
about the sordid truth that is found
in the sad song of the night crow.

## The Fledgling

From out of the bushes
came a mewling cry
followed by another
bird's calm reply.

The fledgling crying,
"The world is too big
I feel so exposed
sitting here on this twig.

The world it is such
a fearsome place
and I lack the power
of your stately grace

What shall I do?
I don't want to die
but I am so small
and that is why I cry."

And the adult bird
landed on a twig above
gazing down with
a mother's love

*"Hush little birdie*
*don't you cry*
*there's nothing to fear*
*and I'll tell you why."*

And chirping on
in a soothing way
finding the right
things to say

*"Yes, the world is big
but you can have it all
if you listen carefully
you can hear its call."*

"Tell me the secret
what can it be
the dangers of this world
are overwhelming me

It hasn't been long
since I left the egg
all I've learned so far
is how to beg,"

*"There is no reason
that you should fear
you have the power,
let me make it clear*

*You have wings
so you can fly,
flex them now
and find the sky."*

## Gray Day Introspection

Sitting by the water under a threatening sky
The wind is strong, the tide is high
    And I in empty solitude
Watch all my days go drifting by

I am not in control of this trip
I am not the captain of this ship
    Suddenly the weather takes a turn
And dark clouds begin to drip

Nothing accomplished, nothing done
Wind blown and alone by the river run
    The day and I a sullen gray
Thick clouds smothering the sun

High above jet planes flying
Soaring gulls all are crying
    Battered by the winds of change
The day and I slowly dying

Exhausted by the human race
I find myself in last place
    Feeling uniquely alone
Rain drops, like tears, staining my face.

## Fingers and Lips

Fingers and lips in two places at once
the mind in the fiction of desire
words cannot suffice this night
and the spirit too soon will expire

Breathing and breath, a gasp and a sigh
flesh still holding the warmth of the day
the moment passes, the silence collapses
and words seem inadequate to say

The darkness incomplete as shapes stir
bed springs have stopped complaining
the mind digests new memories
and outside the night is raining

A hug and a kiss after the moment of bliss
empty and lost in the dreams of a dunce
newfound memories rewound and replayed
of fingers and lips in two places at once.

## NUTSHELL

It came a little closer today
than it usually does, its nearness
a subtlety implied and implicit
the hair and teeth of closeness
the fur and fang of love
feasting on the flesh
of its urgent immediacy
the smoke and cloud
of soul and self
a tightening circle
a decaying orbit
a needle getting closer
to the end of the song
a second skin proximate
physically close
emotionally distant
the hardness meant for
keeping out or holding in
the armor of wizened age
becomes life in a nutshell.

## DAY ON THE BAY

Sun Fish regatta
glinting in the sun
like origami swans
in a slow ballet
and they set the pace
for today's existence
with the rhythm
of their dance
and in their grace
I find peace
until darkness falls
when I will sail to
an island of light
dropping anchor
at the bar for my
daily ration of rum
although I wouldn't
say no to a Guinness
even though I've never
been out on the water.

## INTO THE VORTEX

Swirling, spinning
Hypnotic descent
Into the madness
Of your pretense

A graphic display
Of the final fall
A downward spiral
Into nothing at all

A mental plunge
A psychotic break
Far too much
For a mind to take

And then you're gone
A victim of the vertigo
And all you've learned
Is what you do not know.

## Oblivious

Welcome to oblivion
third planet from desire
orbiting endlessly around
the eternally burning fire

From the ooze of despair
feral and untamed
naked of any virtue
not easily shamed

The gravity of depression
the hurt I can't forget
fifty stories up above
working without a net

Oblivious of the past
with a future to be feared
it's obvious to anyone
who hasn't disappeared

So, welcome to oblivion
have you come to stay?
Despite what you may have heard
nothing's worth the price you have to pay.

## Unwinding

The past is made from the bones
of the present, the future
its unborn child


The continuing family of time
the innate continuity of clan
based on the taming of the wild

•

Death is an undoing
a grave is a gateway
between the worlds of love and fate


Woman to man, man to woman
is the natural human dynamic
of how we all relate

•

Time is like the flower's
unwinding Spring spiral
symbol of eternity spinning

Love is its heart

soul is its faith

all else is useful for sinning

•

I stopped and smelled a rose

I suppose it's what one does

in order to relax

But the perfume wasn't there

only the emptiness of air

but then came a profusion of lilacs

•

What is old is never new again

what is now is quickly fading

what is to come is the great unknown

Bees fly between flowers

from honey-heavy hives

all through the fading hours

wherever time has flown.

## BEAUTY IS

As the twig is bent
So the tree will grow
And sometimes beauty
Is the devil you know

Beauty isn't always
What meets the eye
The Elephant Man
Was a human bonsai

We twist our lives
Into odd paradigms
Seeking forgiveness
For imaginary crimes

Poetry is the rhythm
Of a human heart
Another heart's respnse
Is how words become art

What you see in life
Is seldom what you get
Sometimes beauty is
The ugly you forget.

## The Gambler

The lottery machine
just rejected my dollar
you can't win if you don't pay
but in Bingo you get to holler

Poverty again assured
embrace the status quo
the gains will be ill gotten
from any dice you throw

Random numbers on the screen
but none are the ones you chose
and the horse that you picked in the race
lost by the length of its formidable nose

What use this losing streak
what use this dollar bill
a fool who trusts in luck
never wins and never will.

## STRING THEORY

Strings get pulled
    and the puppet jerks
that's just the way
    the puppet works

And we are conditioned
    in how we react
to every promise
    posed as fact

And we believe
    as we know we must
taught to accept
    and trained to trust

The illusion of free will
    and the cage unlatched
but nothing is ever free
    that has strings attached.

## LAST OF THE SUMMER ROSES

A few days into Summer
and the roses have passed
their petals, heavy with rain,
stain the sidewalk like
drops of blood.
 While beside the fading bush
the lilac buds are bursting
into glorious blossoms.
 And a mixture of sadness
and happiness grips me
and the familiar air of ennui
in a state of mournful joy
leaving me feeling unfulfilled.
 Although the sadness is
perhaps a little stronger
leaving an aftertaste
like a sip of cheap wine.
 And the acid of grief
rises in the back of my throat
and I weep over the dying roses
as bleeding petals
fall at my feet.

## Twenty-Five Shades of Gray

A medium hue gray gull soaring
against the bright light of a gray sky
above darker gray waters, sets the tone

Gray mist clings to body and soul
moored boats of the lightest gray
bob idly in the gray of dreams

Brain's gray cells idle too
in the dull gray of memory
and the aching gray of age

Gray, weathered wooden piers
rise and fall on tall gray pilings
as gray fog gathers on the datk gray bay

The gray notes of a sad song
hang in the heavy gray air
of this gun-metal gray Sunday

Gray, crushed shells protest underfoot
the light of day a sullen gray
and gray buildings shiver on the shore

Fractured gray reflections dance
beside the gray, granite sea wall
built of every shade of gray stone
a gray hardness on this soft, gray day.

## ISLAND IN THE SUN

Slab work

functional and prosaic.

Form built and squared

dry sand, cement

and pebbles for strength

in an old wheelbarrow

formed into a cratered mound

and water added

mixed by hand

with shovel and hoe

the gritty scritch and scratch

sofening into a thick, viscous mass

carefully poured into the mold

like primal mud, left to set.

Slurry rising to the top

like cream to be skimmed

the mixture stiffens into its repose

into the promise of its strength.

Now comes the hardest part,

resisting the temptation

to tamper and smooth

and the urge to add

a name or initials

or a hand or foot print,

maybe just the date,

small, in the corner

a simple sign of pride

for patience rewarded.

The form is stripped

revealing the final shape

and you are left with

the permanence of

a place to stand

and sing its praises

on your island in the sun.

## What Occurs

Somewhere over the rainbow
far from the hue and cry
in the far flung fields of Elysium
there is a place for you and I

It's no good to wish upon a star
the future has been foretold
just because you are aging
doesn't mean that you are old

The wandering chimney smoke
speaks to us of times gone by
sometimes tears are sadness
sometimes just a cinder in your eye

And high upon a mountain top
the air too thin to catch a breath
the wise man took a step toward God
and plummeted to his death

And in the moment of his falling
the secret of life was his to keep
though love may be the answer
always look before you leap.

## LIQUID SKY

The water is a liquid sky
where featherless fish can fly

•

The ribbon of the river free
unwinding to adorn the sea

•

The river is an estuary wide
coming and going with the tide

•

The sky above, the mud below
and in between the tidal flow

•

The air is thin above the solid cloud
and down here life is lived out loud

•

The bird, the bee, the wind, the wave
entertain us in the ways they behave

•

And far away I see a patch of blue
above the water passing through

•

From where I sit with jaundiced eye
contemplating the liquid sky.

## THE HERESY OF NOW

        An old itch re-scratched.
I have read the books
each one three or four times
fifteen volumes in all and
the me of now has gotten
everything that can be gotten
from their decaying pages.
If I should revisit them
at some far distant time
would an older me
be able to glean more
or would it be no more
than a mere remembrance?

        An old itch re-scratched.
For some people time does not exist
it is not a flowing stream
but a now, flowing without restraint
needing only its own immediacy.
To read the books a hundred times
would bring no advancement
beyond the heresy of now.
With no idea of what a future is,
and the past a fractured myth,
the very act of reading seems
to be lacking any valid reason
vis-á-vis the pertinence of now.

## THE ROCKER

On the rocker the widow's glove
having lost its grip on love
lies disconsolate and alone

The mattress still holds the shape
of her old body in the rut of her years
where she left an enduring impression

She had loved only once in life
but she had loved well
until her love was taken from her

She rocked back and forth
in the rhythm of that love
cradling his body with her mind

She never moved on but lived
in that moment until there were
no more moments left to live

And now the empty rocker
on the porch where she dreamed
sometimes rocks in the breeze
with love smiling in its caress.

## MY AGE IS WINTER

    My age is Winter
barren cold in mid-July
bitter wind of infirmities
sun dispensing pity
in golden dollops
a useless lozenge
against the ills of age.

    My age is Winter
a life lacking endurance
and clarity of thought
more and more
life is less and less.
Grown from nothingness
that it now returns to.

    My age is Winter
old as the age of reason
older than any season
time is only sun and moon
only the passing of the days
leaving seconds, minutes and hours
for the young to spend.

    My age is Winter
empty, slow and gray.
Love the only warmth
the heart will allow
and that a fading ember
in the fading days
of the Winter of my age.

## How Now

Here in the now of when
lost in the now and then
both exist as where you've been
now is the time for all good men

It's now or never, I hear you say
never lacks a now and so you stay
where you are in the here and now
it's easy to do, once you know how

Here, in this very moment of time
thinking thoughts of now sublime
which is neither here nor there
but in the moment they both share

How now brown cow? As if it knew
a question asked since now was new
the how is easy, it's now that's hard
now is a fight with no holds barred.

## Tower builders

We build towers to our egos
and weep when those towers fall.

•

Height is our metaphor for success
and these monuments to money
are meant to cast the long shadows
of our phallic greatness.

•

Why build a slab on the ground
when you can build an arrow
to pierce the sky.

•

Some towers are raised to God
some razed by the godless
but none rise above who we are.

•

We celebrate their points of view
the vast panoramas they afford.
Tall, tiered hives of busy people
in the constant buzz of commerce.

•

It's simple economics
it's cheaper to build vertically
than to build horizontally;
taller rather than wider.
Land must be bought
while the sky is free.

      •

And there, in the aeries of eagles
nearer to the gods of Olympus
at the border of the clouds
these man-made mountains rise
like all towers in history;
into the air, but not of the air.

      •

The language of the tower builders
does not speak to human scale,
but more like Jack's ill-fated beanstalk.
When we build towers to our egos
we then see those towers fall.

## KNEE JERKS

Paint a rainbow on your face
Notre Dame's in second place
March is mad, the people too
We wonder what would Jesus do

Dust and ash have settled now
Grief has furrowed every brow
Take down the flag that speaks of race
Strike the colors of disgrace

Another day, another slaughter
Air is poisoned, so too the water
Death will follow every birth
Who is left to save the earth

Hail Mary, full of Grace
Notre Dame's still in second place
Bless us Father for we sin
Give us this day that we can win.

## Vacuous Vacuum

In the vacuous vacuum of the day
thoughts like curdled cream
rising to the conscious
from a subconscious dream

Idleness of thought is a busy thing
it keeps the mind up working late
a million thoughts at a constant boil
hoping some of them will percolate

Thoughts stew in the waters of life
and from its brew I drink my fill
just because I know I can
it's logical that I think I will

These thoughts beyond my control
coming from such an utter wretch
it's a wonder those who dare to drink
would ever taste such a bitter vetch.

## The Fourth

Beyond where I can see, a celebration
of life and liberty is going on
overhead, helicopters and planes circle
looking for a body lost at sea

Search boats also ply
the flat expanse of bay
searching for the man
who didn't come home yesterday

He had threatened to harm himself
anchored his boat and took a swim
two days they have searched
but there is still no sign of him

Tonight a fireworks display
will light up the evening sky
in their glory we're left to wonder
why anyone should wish to die

And in the midst of life
we are made aware of death
and so embrace the preciousness
of the now of every breath.

## LEONARDO

Da Vinci studied bats and gulls in flight
before designing his ornithopter
but, he, himself, never flew

With only brush and paint
he captured the definitive smile
though he, himself, seldom did

He was an equal opportunity lover
who hid his thoughts in mirror writing
but, he, himself, was an open book

He invented cannons and tanks
and refined the art of war
but, he, himself, was a man of peace

He was a genius of contradictions
a man with few enemies and fewer friends
but, he, himself, sought out neither

He painted mostly religious themes
and like every man he believed in God
but he believed in himself more as a creator
painting himself bestowing life on Adam.

## SOMETHING

Everything is hunting something
Everyone is haunted by something
Something tells me that I don't know
Why everybody hides from something

Some things are better left unsaid
Some messages are better left unread
Put it back in the bottle, put it back in the sea
Sometimes the message isn't meant for me

Everything means something to somebody
Something is nothing if left unsaid
Some things are sometimes better than other things
If something dies, it doesn't mean it's dead

Sometimes it's the something you lose
Sometimes it's the something you find
And sometimes you're really something
Needing something to help you unwind

Something is anything that comes from nothing
Or something that comes from some thing
Or it's nothing that you mistook for something
Something is usually better than nothing

But sometimes something is the same thing
And the something we wished for isn't always
The something that we manage to somehow find
Serendipity is the something you weren't hunting

It just goes to show, it's always something
Something on the tip of your tongue,
Something in the back of your mind
Something you always wanted to say.

## Alphabetical

Ailing
Boa
Constrictor
Dies
Eating
Fetid
Guinea
Hen.
Infected
Jackal
Killed
Licking
Messy
Noxious
Offal.
Pigs
Quickly
Retching
Sickly.
Tasting
Useless
Vise
Wrapped
Xerophilous
Young
Zebra.

## WHAT WAS EASY

What was easy, that now is hard
Which stirred the heart to love
Transmuted now without regard
For feelings of the raven for the dove

The language spoken lacks the voice
To articulate true passion's worth
Or to effectively refute the choice
That dooms love to roam the earth

The ties loosened and let slip
A new journey begun alone
The shore deserted by the ship
Seeking where the dove has flown

Nothing matters when you're dead
You only have the here and now
To sail a different voyage instead
But never quite knowing how.

## Shopping Cart

Bright orange and yellow
toy, plastic shopping cart
loud against the dying grass
abandoned by the little girl
in the corner of her yard
askew, forlorn and empty.
Struck by a shaft of sunlight
like a spotlight on a dream
an abandoned game unfinished
imaginary groceries
faded like memories
wheels sunk in rain damp grass
her laughter stilled
her father's bellow
fading on the breeze
plastic shopping cart
the brightness of it mocking
the dark days passage
nothing depending on it
glazed with rainwater
signifying nothing.

## HALF-LIGHT

Peering through the dark puzzle

of branches and leaves

to the sunlit flowered field

it's easy to dismiss the half-lit world

as an uninteresting frame

for the field's bright beauty.

But when an artist paints the scene

he shows the equal truth of both

and although it's true, the eye

is drawn to color and light,

the soul revels in the half-light

of shadows where love

so often finds release.

## Becoming

The thought you think
is the now you have
memories are the bones
of thoughts interred
and the thoughts of the future
are still only thoughts of now.

The thoughts you think
that you build upon
to become the tomorrow
of your imagination
immediate and fleeting
are still only thoughts of now.

The moments you think of as past
are memories in the museum of thought
the bones of thoughts wearing
the flesh of dreams dancing
in the light of probability
are still only thoughts of now.

Thoughts are a private thing
unknowable, unreadable
personal journeys through
the landscapes of the mind
what manifests in this mirror
are still only thoughts of now.

Thoughts, once written down,
become the poetry of self
the self of now becoming the who
you are and were and will be
and poems spoken thoughtfully
are still only thoughts of now.

The thought you think
is the now you have
you live with those thoughts
and what seems sometimes to be
thoughtless random musings
are still only thoughts of now.

## FLAGSTUFF

We fly flags of our biography
on our boats, poles and bodies
extolling country, cause and hobbies
each in their singular iconography

Romans had standards that they flew
flags and banners emblazoned SPQR
so wave a checkered flag for the winning car
and hoist the glory of the red, white and blue

The Crusades had their cross to bear
while Hitler adopted a broken one
and before the Japanese flew the rising sun
pirate's Jolly Roger was flapping in the air

Tattooed skin can be a flag of sorts
as are the colored bandanas of street gangs
the balanced symmetry of Yins and Yangs
and colorful rings of Olympic sports

# SONG OF THE NIGHT CROW — Christopher J. Roe

Dying for the flag is a price we sometimes pay
wrapping ourself in the politics of it
or killing imagined enemies in the name of it
or just waving the rainbows of the gay

They've been planted on the moon
and sent into the deepness of outer space
they are the way we define our place
as we sing another patriotic tune

You can drape it over a soldier's coffin
or shoot at 18 of them, if golf's your game
or in protest you can burn it in anger's flame
because wars are happening far too often

You can wave it from a bunting-draped grand stand
as a patriot or a bigot, it's sometimes hard to tell
the black and white blind faith of heaven or hell
is something that I neither salute nor understand.

## QUESTIONS OF LONELINESS

Do all the people I meet in my world
really exist, or do I imagine them
to fill the lonely days?

Sometimes they seem to be characters
in an obtuse play entering and exiting
while speaking their lines

When I go through a door, do I exchange
one reality for another, or is it all the same
reality that someone's put a door in?

If every exit is an entrance to someplace else
doesn't that mean they are all entrances
and exits just don't exist?

I tend to over-think things too much
maybe I should call an imaginary friend
to join me for a drink, and is that then
an entrance, or an exit strategy?

## ONLY THE LONELY

A sultry night, window open,
but no refreshing breeze
to cool the troubled soul.
Couples walk by, conversing,
their voices an unwanted
reminder of my solitude.
The moon, nearly full,
stares down, like a lidded eye,
glaring at me, judgmentally.
It hangs there, all alone,
the sky empty, but for the moon,
lonely, as am I.
I take a walk, saying hello
to people that I meet
my voice sounds odd
in the heavy, humid, air.
I say good bye too, wondering,
if any of them even care.
Some people answer, some do not,
and I hear myself sigh, the way
lonely people do, when they think
about the hopelessness of it all
on a sultry night, window open,
but no refreshing breeze.

## In the mirror world

In the mirror world
you can see everything
but there is no sound
it is a silent place

A mirror bounces light
capturing, color and motion
I look in from my noisy world
but there is no sound

If the mirror could reflect sound
would words come out backwards
would meanings be reversed
but there is no sound

The people I see in the mirror
behind the mirrored me, jump about
their reflections dancing to unheard music
but there is no sound

## SONG OF THE NIGHT CROW — *Christopher J. Roe*

Light, color, movement

not music, not voices, not noise

only the captured dance

but there is no sound


Does the me in the mirror see them

dancing behind me though I'm alone

I can see them dancing behind him

but there is no sound


When those in the mirror look out

at their backwards selves, what do they

make of all the noise we make

but there is no sound


When I turn out the light to go to bed

in the corner of my eye the light in the mirror

still burns and I see a face screamimg

but there is no sound.

## The Following

Blessed are the meek
who stooped to smell the roses
the parting of the water
showed the way to Moses
and the dove held a branch in its beak

I never really thought like them
their thoughts like fireflies in a jar
like lambs to the slaughter
following the light of a distant star
on the road to Bethlehem

All down the Via Dolorosa road
where he bore the burden of his grief
I serve my penance in a bar
it has tempered my belief
that nothing borrowed is nothing owed

Let the sinner be the saint
let each of us find our inner peace
to find out who we really are
follow the arrow of flying geese
to the promised land, old and quaint

In the communion of body and blood
beyond where the waters part
where fireflies are winking in a jar
in the shadow of the sacred heart
let the two of us ride out the flood

Blessed are the meek
who stooped to smell the roses
for they never stoop too far
finding love right under their noses
and what hides, they must seek.

## THE PINK SCREEN

Eyes tightly closed
and upon the pink screen
dark shapes float across
the sky of your eye.
Move your eyes
back and forth and up and down
and the shapes dart and drift,
rise and fall in their
Newtonian ballet.
These captured motes,
tiny wingless angels
seeking the heaven
of their dreams
on the pink screen of your eyes,
the gateway to your soul
and the water of your tears,
the river Styx.

## BIG LESSON

The small blind dog
is oblivious to its blindness
adapting to, and accepting of,
each day as it comes.
*This is what today is.*
*This is how I'll live it.*
Dogs don't regret or wish
they don't reflect on their lot
with no concept of fate
they either exist, or they do not.
Guided and cared for
by a loving master;
a friend of many years
the dog lives its life,
neither slower nor faster,
as a dog should
without rancor or tears
and what it can't see
it smells or hears.
That is the big lesson
of the small blind dog.

## DARK SOUL
*for C.K.*

    Dark art
morbid canvases
marginalized
shapes
    isolated
        non-reactive
            alone
Colors of melancholy
    and pain
        Islands
of collective depression
arranged on the walls
    A morose gallery
        of weeping paint
The art could not heal
    the colors could not soothe
        the mind cried out
but the world was deaf
    The artist
hung his paintings
    and then he
        hung himself.

## MID

Midship; the stablest part of the ship
Middle child; usually the stablest child
Midnight; the witching hour
Midday; siesta, the sleeping hour
Middlebrow; a poem that is not highbrow
Middle Earth; a place of pure fantasy
Middleman; between the idea and the deal
Midwife; between the womb and the world
Midwifery; between the dream and the reality
Midsummer; the solstice of dreams
Middling; just a little way from fair
Midgard; the dry land that we inhabit
Middle of the road; the least confrontational stand
Midstream; no place to switch horses
Mid-air; a bad place to collide
Midden; a steaming pile of crap
Middle finger; an irreverent salute
Middle Class; not poor, not rich, but footing the bill
Middlescence; being old, but acting young
Midlife crisis; the sudden realization you are old
Middle-aged; the point between youth and wisdom
Middle Ages; the dark before the light
Midbrain; the mesencephalon, or primitive brain
Midway; two islands in the middle of the sea
Middle C; the perfect pitch of my scream.

## AS THE MIND SIGHS

The artist in a malaise of introspection
hating what he's doing, hating what he's done
like all artists at some point, wallowing in self-pity

He has been saying what he had to say
but in the end what did he really have to say
that hadn't already been said by others

A new idea begins to form and it feels promising
in his mind he sees a potential personal masterpiece
that in reality he knows will fail in its attempt

And yet he pushes on knowing that the best works
always comes as a surprise, while the bad works
sadly are not surprising, but predictable

But that is the ancient curse of the artist
because, with the vision comes the pain
and the downward spiral into madness

    As the mind sighs

And in the absence of creativity's light
in the darkness and the loathing
he waits patiently, talking to his ghosts

He stares with open eyes that do not see
with a mind slowly being dulled by age
the artist examines the ectoplasm of thought

For no reason, he thinks of different animals that spit
the llama and the camel, as does a certain cobra,
and man, but then he loses his train of thought

He's trying not to think about life's palette;
Payne's Gray, Burnt Umber, Prussian Blue,
Dioxazine Purple and the Black of the void

A fading artist once quick and bright
desperately seeking self-realization
sucking on the marrow of his soul
for the nourishment of self-esteem

    As the mind sighs.

## THE GREATER QUESTION

Lately I have grown weary
most of my work is done
and what now is labororius
is what once was fun


Does the world need another painting
does it need yet another poem
what will it all add up to but
another hefty, rhyme-riddled tome


For all of my working life
I have been nothing if not prolific
producing mostly generalities
but nothing too specific


I suppose the greater question is
do I really need to keep working
in the dark recesses of my intellect
is there a masterpiece lurking

How much more can I do for love
before familiarity proves contemptible
quitting while I'm ahead
seems far more sensible

But I didn't get this far based
on the strength of my sanity alone
something else must be at work here
there must be seeds yet to be sown

True, most of my work is done
but there's still a bit more to do
still words to rhyme, paint to mix
before I'm finally through.

## BOILER ROOM

In the hot steamy fog of the boiler room
that is my brain, a lone, gray figure
shovels coal into the fiery red maw
to feed the hungry, burning furnace

There are a host of pipes and plumbing
sweat faced gauges with jittery arrows
and a red emergency shut-off button
like a cherry tomato in a garden of steam

The gray figure glistens with exertion
the shovel glints in the fire's glow
and the thought machine chugs along
firing off synapses somewhere down the line

Too many neurotransmitters going off at once
a sensory overload of unchecked thoughts
the red-hot furnace develops a balloon-like bulge
looking like something in an old cartoon

Steam begins to shoot from the sudden cracks
the gray figure drops his coal-laden shovel
looking frantically in the over-heated steam cloud
for the glowing red cherry tomato of salvation.

## Cyclopean

Staring into the cyclopean eye
beyond the orchard's pursed lips
quivering tongue and fingertips
dancing on the breath of a sigh

Gazing into the yawning abyss
into the bottomless pit of love
the gift below from the one above
bestowing a parting kiss

Part and plunge
like a deep sea diver
a sexual survivor
absorbing love like a sponge

Deep, deep into the chasm
exploring the holy cave
as love's enduring slave
savoring the orgasm.

## A RELIGIOUS EXPERIENCE

Swirling brown clouds
like darkening storms
above the emerging black
a priest's collar forms

Offering salvation
to the chosen few
dark companion
to Tullamore Dew

The storms keep coming
all night long
what feels so right
just can't be wrong

The crowning touch
of the real McCoy
the remaining brain cells
that we destroy

The golden harp
the heavenly choir

in the stormy glass
that we desire

Such are the miracles
so righteous and pure
the cross we bear
our nightly cure

And it all starts
with the holy brew
from St. James Gate
in a pint or two

The monsoon clouds
in the parting glass
the magic elixir
helping the night to pass

The too-short evening
of the swirling snow
the only religion
we need to know.

## OF FLOWERS AND LOVE

The poet describes the flower
the bursting sheath, the spreading petals
equating it to an act of love
when the hovering bee settles

The bee that penetrates
and the dew after the rains
the pulsing red of the rose
and the pollen that stains

The throat of the lily
the perfume of excess
the hummingbird's tongue
the flowers we press

The wilting and dying
after the seed is spread
gathered flower bouquet
to honor the dead

Allegory and metaphor like
the nevermore of the raven quoth
the poet writes of flowers and love
misunderstanding both.

## PRIVILEGE & POWER

A religion that calls for one's death
or the death of others whom you've never met
is less a religion than a despotic dictatorship

It's about privilege and power
the gaining of one and wielding of the other
afterlife's promises are the whip of control

Most of the world's religions are monotheistic
but are those hundreds of gods really one
operating under their assumed names?

Churches, temples, mosques
are all places of worship that you'd think
would be more understanding

But the devil of privilege and power
demands conformity to the rules
in effect, refuting God's existence

Whatever book or symbol you use, remember,
belief is a learned behavior, a conditioned response
to a lifetime of lessons, and it is not God who calls,
but the, unchallenged, who claim to speak for Him.

## The running man

He couldn't outrun his past
time flies, the past flies fast
he couldn't outdistance what he'd done
no matter how far he tried to run

•

Sky as lusterous as a pearl
wind the soft breath of a girl
nights die as days are born
the runner runs his path well worn

•

He no longer runs, he's grown too old
his past a story his shame has retold
the running man has gone to ground
and all he has left is what he's found

•

It's not enough, but he can run no more
it's hard to remember what he was running for
the horizon burns with the day's new promise
in the stillness, the past stops by to reminisce.

## THE LARGE BARKING DOG

Next door, the large dog barks all day
in the window of the empty apartment
a prisoner calling, "Out, out, out"

Is the message it's trying to coney
I can't explain its sour temperament
and I quiet it for a while with a shout

Who really knows what a dog is thinking
in the abject boredom of its primitive mind
it barks the same "word" over and over

Its throat parched, I hear it drinking
from a bowl the owner left behind
that bears the name of Rover

Other dogs wander past in the park
and a frantic conversation ensues
with a lot of peeing against the trees

All day long I hear the large dog bark
praying it will tire soon and snooze
perhaps it's been driven mad by fleas.

## THE HOUSE OF LOVE

Distance is the house of love
silent with memories of you
thoughts and dreams feed
the moments passing through

You cannot fill a broken cup
its emptiness is the face of fate
the love that came and went
and the love that came too late

The heart still holds on to love
thoughts become the cup
warmth of what might have been
not enough to fill it up

Absence is a constant void
distance is the house of love
where thoughts and dreams recall
the heart of the absent dove.

## Versus

As the drab world floats by
are you swimming or sinking?

•

In the harshness of your life
are you lying down or wounded?

•

In the midst of your daily struggles
are you flying or falling?

•

After a long, arduous day
are you yawning or screaming?

•

Seeking solace in a glass
are you happy or just drunk?

•

Is the quick black and white blinking
the movie of your life passing?

•

Are your eyes opened to see
or have you slipped into a coma?

•

And finlly, the last question,
is it sleep or is it death?

## LAST OF THE DIEHARD SMOKERS

Out in the cold and rain
bundled up against wind and snow
stamping feet and coughing
behind the cigarette's red glow

Returning to the bar
sniffling from the cold
looking for a reason
not to grow old

And in the quiet bar
listening to whistling breaths
like worn out tires going flat
in slow, lingering deaths

In the evening of their sorrows
tiny red warning lights blinking
the last of the diehard smokers light up
the time they have left shrinking.

## A MODERN MAN

In the future I envision
there stands a crooked tree
its ripened fruit falling
in great prolificacy

In its branches a serpent twined
but I am not tempted by calls
of the fruit or the serpent
and the fruit rots where it falls

The serpent sheds its skin
like a lacy negligee
becoming a beautiful woman
made of song and clay

A flower in her tumbling hair
the bees are moving slow
gorging on the rotting pulp
and the garden is aglow

I step into its paradise
naked and newborn
a modern man claiming
the welcome he's outworn.

## Passion & persistence

Somewhere beyond the boundaries
of brain storms and dreams
existing on the cusp of imagination
or at least, that's how it seems

In the twilight shadows of desire
living a life of compromise
aching for the sunlit twinkles
dancing in the muse's eyes

Where memories become realities
and promises are made into a meal
what determines how you live
are the passions that you feel

Love is a long held hope
the very fuel that keeps life going
far off where the darkness looms
the light of love is softly glowing

The heart pumps warming blood
and the brain responds to stimuli
love plucks the edges of awareness
where hopes and dreams are made to fly

And soaring on that imagination
to wherever the heart wants to go
life is less about who you meet
as who you come to know

Doors open and doors close
sometimes you walk through
not so much to find love
as to allow love to find you

Somewhere beyond the boundaries
of where fate has chosen to exist
coming alive in passion's moment
where hopes and dreams persist.

Made in the USA
Lexington, KY
23 September 2015